KT-419-132

barbecues

barbecues

This edition first published in the U.K. in 2000 by Hamlyn for WHSmith, Greenbridge Road, Swindon SN3 3LD

Copyright © 2000 Octopus Publishing Group Limited

Octopus Publishing Group Limited
2–4 Heron Quays
London E14 4JP

ISBN 0 600 60030 0

Printed in China

Quote used with the kind permission of Sir Clement Freud.

Notes

1 Standard level spoon measurements are used in all recipes.

1 tablespoon = one 15 ml spoon
1 teaspoon = one 5 ml spoon

2 Both imperial and metric measurements have been given in all recipes. Use one set of measurements only and not a mixture of both.

3 Measurements for canned foods have been given as a standard metric equivalent.

4 Eggs should be medium unless otherwise stated. The Department of Health advises that eggs should not be consumed raw. This book may contain dishes made with lightly cooked eggs. It is prudent for more vulnerable people, such as pregnant and nursing mothers, invalids, the elderly, babies and young children, to avoid uncooked or lightly cooked dishes made with eggs. Once prepared, these dishes should be used immediately.

5 Milk should be full fat unless otherwise stated.

6 Poultry should always be cooked thoroughly. To test if poultry is cooked, pierce the flesh through the thickest part with a skewer or fork – the juices should run clear, never pink or red.

7 Fresh herbs should be used unless otherwise stated. If unavailable, use dried herbs as an alternative but halve the quantities stated.

8 Pepper should be freshly ground black pepper unless otherwise stated; season according to taste.

9 Ovens should be preheated to the specified temperature – if using a fan-assisted oven, follow the manufacturer's instructions for adjusting the time and the temperature.

10 Do not re-freeze a dish that has been frozen previously.

11 This book includes dishes made with nuts and nut derivatives. It is advisable for customers with known allergic reactions to nuts and nut derivatives and those who may be potentially vulnerable to these allergies, such as pregnant and nursing mothers, invalids, the elderly, babies and young children, to avoid dishes made with nuts and nut oils. It is also prudent to check the labels of pre-prepared ingredients for the possible inclusion of nut derivatives.

12 Vegetarians should look for the 'V' symbol on a cheese to ensure it is made with vegetarian rennet. There are vegetarian forms of Parmesan, feta, Cheddar, Cheshire, red Leicester, dolcelatte and many goats' cheeses, among others.

From burgers to spare ribs and kebabs to sausages, there is a great selection here for the hungry guest. Marinades, relishes and sauces add to the unique flavour that cooking over charcoal gives to food.

Cajun-style Cod and Spicy Fish Satay are just two of the dishes that you will find in this chapter. Simply cooked fresh fish is both delicious and healthy and with such a great variety of fish and shellfish available, it is an excellent choice for the barbecue.

There is no need for the vegetarian to feel left out at the barbecue, as the versatility of these dishes makes a great alternative to meat and fish. Red Bean & Rice Patties, Stuffed Mini Peppers with Tomato Sauce and Grilled Sweet Potato & Aïoli are all easy to prepare and taste great.

No barbecue is complete without a selection of salads and vegetables and there are plenty to choose from in this chapter. Many of the recipes in this chapter can be prepared in advance, from Warm Sweet Potato and Walnut Salad to Fresh Mayonnaise.

A happy ending is a sweet ending and barbecues are no exception. Try the refreshing Melon & Rosewater Granita to cool the palate on a hot day or the delicious Chocolate & Pine Nut Meringue Stack. Make these desserts in advance to leave plenty of time to relax and enjoy yourself.

contents

introduction

There is nothing quite like the delicious aroma of food grilling on the barbecue to stimulate the appetite. There is always something special about eating in the open air. What is more, everyone wants to help, whether it is turning steaks or ferrying salads from the kitchen to the table.

This book is packed with mouth-watering recipes to help you to make the most of the long summer evenings and sunny weekend afternoons by inviting friends and family over for a barbecue. Barbecues are traditionally centred around meat and poultry so there is a wonderful selection of family favourites as well as plenty of new ideas. Instead of buying ready-made burgers, try making your own unforgettable ones. There are also recipes for home-made sausages as well as delicious kebabs, chops, spare ribs, steaks and chicken breasts.

Fish and seafood are the perfect choice for the barbecue as they cook so rapidly. Delicate fish can be wrapped in foil parcels to preserve both flavour and texture, while more robust types can be cooked directly on the grill or threaded on to skewers. The fabulous fish dishes include recipes for tuna, sardines, snapper, trout, salmon and, of course, prawns.

An increasing number of people are now adding chargrilled and barbecued vegetables to the menu as they are a tasty treat and are also quick and easy to prepare and cook. As well as tried-and-tested favourites, such as potatoes and corn on the cob, there are recipes for patties, kebabs, stuffed peppers and even polenta. Barbecued vegetables may be served in addition to meat or fish or as a vegetarian alternative. If you are cooking for both meat-eaters and vegetarians, look for the recipes where the vegetables are sealed inside foil packets so that they do not come into contact with any meat juices.

No barbecue would be complete without a choice of salads and the variety here is almost endless – cold or warm, tangy or creamy, sweet or spicy, crunchy or melt-in-the mouth. Also included are a number of salad dressings, which can be used exactly as they appear or adapted to suit your particular taste and menu.

There is no need for the barbecue to end once the chops have been demolished and the plates cleared away, as this book contains a superb collection of indulgent desserts. You can choose between preparing summer desserts, ices and sorbets in advance – an ideal solution if you are planning a party – or delicious barbecued fruits.

The barbecue

There is a large choice of barbecues on the market and a wide price range. If you are buying a new barbecue, consider how often you are likely to use it and how many people you will be cooking for. Inexpensive and portable, hibachi barbecues consist of a cast iron 'firebox' with one or more grills which can be raised or lowered to decrease or increase the amount of heat directly on the food. Nowadays, there are also lighter-weight versions as well.

'To barbecue is a way of life rather than a desirable method of cooking.'

Sir Clement Freud

Brazier barbecues, which are slightly more expensive, are a popular choice for patios, balconies and gardens. They usually stand on legs and may have wheels, but are often uncomfortably low if you are cooking for any length of time. The grills may be round or rectangular and come in a range of sizes. The grill height is usually adjustable and extras may include a spit, shelf and hood.

Kettle barbecues are usually much more expensive, but extremely adaptable and efficient. A large domed lid may be used to turn the barbecue into an 'oven' for cooking whole chickens and joints of meat. As it is usually hinged, it can also be used as a windbreak when you are grilling. The heat is controlled by air vents. They tend to stand at a more comfortable height than braziers and usually have wheels.

The ultimate choice is a built-in barbecue. Kits are available from many DIY stores, where firebricks can also be purchased. Choose a sheltered site with easy access to the kitchen.

Disposable and portable barbecues are also available for occasional use and for picnics. The former consists of a foil tray, already packed with fuel and a lightweight grill. They will last for about an hour and are good for picnics. Portable barbecues are more robust, but still lightweight enough to transport easily. They will fold flat to fit in the boot of a car.

Gas barbecues are becoming increasingly popular. They are expensive, but the heat is instant and easily controlled and they are easy to keep clean. However, food cooked in this way does not have the traditional barbecue flavour.

Lighting the barbecue

Charcoal is the most common type of fuel that is used to light the barbecue as it gives a long-lasting and intense heat. Lumpwood, generally made from softwood and in pieces of varying size, is easy to light, but tends to burn away quite quickly. Briquettes burn for a long time and with little smoke, but are often difficult to light. Hardwoods, such as oak and apple, may also be used, but these require constant attention. Their great advantage is their lovely smell. Woodchips and herbs may be scattered over charcoal to create a similar pleasant aroma.

You will need to light the barbecue about 45 minutes–1 hour before you want to start cooking. First, line the base of the barbecue with a layer of foil, which not only reflects the heat, but makes clearing up easier afterwards. Once lit, spread the coals out evenly over the base and leave until they are covered with a film of grey ash before starting to cook.

Safety tips

- Make sure the barbecue is standing steady and never leave a lighted barbecue without supervision. Keep pets and children away.
- Never add liquid firelighter or other flammable materials once the fire is alight and do not attempt to move the barbecue itself.
- Always have a bucket of water and a first aid kit handy in case the worst happens.
- Keep food cold and indoors until you are ready to cook it. Alternatively, keep it in a cool box. Keep raw and cooked food separate.
- Always use long-handled implements, such as tongs and forks, and do not use the same tools for handling raw and cooked food. Oven gloves are also useful.
- Drain food that has been marinating and trim excess fat before cooking to avoid flare-ups.
- Timings in the recipes are approximate, as barbecues will vary. Always check that meat, especially, sausages, burgers and poultry, is cooked through by piercing the thickest part with a fork or the point of a sharp knife. If the juices run clear, the meat is ready, but if there is any trace of pink, then further cooking is required.

meat & poultry

mediterranean lamb cakes with salsa verde

1 Place the lamb, garlic, Parmesan, olives, basil, lemon rind, pine nuts and egg white in a bowl and mix well with a fork. Season with pepper. Shape with wet hands into 8 even-sized patties.

2 Mix together all the salsa ingredients in a bowl. For a smooth salsa, process the ingredients in a food processor or blender and season with salt and pepper to taste.

3 Cook the lamb cakes on the oiled grill of a preheated barbecue for 6–8 minutes on each side, until charred and firm. Serve with the salsa and garnish with mint sprigs.

■ Do not prepare the salsa more than an hour in advance, otherwise the avocado will discolour and it will look unappetizing.

500 g (1 lb) lean minced lamb

2 garlic cloves, crushed

1 tablespoon grated Parmesan cheese

1 tablespoon chopped pitted olives

1 tablespoon chopped basil

finely grated rind of 1 lemon

1 tablespoon chopped, roasted pine nuts

1 egg white

pepper

mint sprigs, to garnish

Salsa Verde:

3 tablespoons chopped parsley

2 tablespoons chopped mint

1 tablespoon chopped chives

4 tablespoons olive oil

1 tablespoon chopped capers

3 garlic cloves, crushed

juice of 1 lemon

1 small onion, chopped

1 ripe avocado, peeled, pitted and chopped

few drops of Tabasco sauce

salt and pepper

Serves 4

Preparation time: 25 minutes

Cooking time: 12–16 minutes

beef & onion kebabs

1. Put all the ingredients for the Chinese Marinade in a screw-top jar and shake well to mix.

2. Thread the cubed beef, onion quarters and mushrooms alternately on to presoaked wooden or oiled metal skewers. Place the skewers in a shallow dish and pour the marinade over. Turn to coat the kebabs thoroughly with the marinade. Cover and leave to marinate for 4 hours in a cool place, turning occasionally.

3. Prepare the tzatziki. Place the cucumber in a colander set over a bowl and sprinkle with salt. Leave to drain for 30 minutes. Rinse the cucumber and pat dry with kitchen paper. Put the cucumber into a bowl and add the yogurt, mint, garlic and salt and pepper. Stir well. Cover and chill.

4. Remove the kebabs from the marinade and reserve the marinade. Cook the kebabs on the oiled grill of a preheated barbecue for about 6–8 minutes, turning once and basting frequently with the reserved marinade. Serve with the tzatziki and boiled rice, if liked.

■ Soaking wooden skewers in cold water for 30 minutes before using them helps to prevent them from charring on the barbecue.

375 g (12 oz) beef topside, cut into 2.5 cm (1 inch) cubes

4 small onions, quartered

16 button mushrooms

mint sprigs, to garnish

boiled rice, to serve (optional)

Chinese Marinade:

2 tablespoons clear honey

4 tablespoons dark soy sauce

4 tablespoons hoisin sauce

1 teaspoon white wine vinegar

8 tablespoons chicken stock

¼ teaspoon Chinese five spice powder

2.5 cm (1 inch) piece fresh root ginger, peeled and finely chopped

Tzatziki:

½ cucumber, peeled and finely diced

150 ml (¼ pint) Greek yogurt

2 tablespoons finely chopped mint

1 garlic clove, crushed

salt and pepper

Serves 4

Preparation time: 10 minutes, plus marinating and draining

Cooking time: 6–8 minutes

beef burgers

1 Mix the beef burger ingredients in a bowl. Form into 6 cakes using a 5 cm (2 inch) scone cutter.

2 Mix the basting ingredients together in a bowl, if using.

3 Cook the beef burgers on the oiled grill of a preheated barbecue for about 5 minutes on each side. Brush with the basting mixture while the beef burgers are grilling.

4 Serve the burgers on hamburger buns with a salad garnish and with the diced and sliced avocado, gherkins, tomato ketchup, onion rings and garnish with paprika.

500 g (1 lb) minced beef

1 green pepper, cored, deseeded and chopped

1 garlic clove, crushed

2 spring onions, finely chopped

2 tablespoons chopped parsley

large pinch of paprika, plus extra, to garnish

salt and pepper

To Baste: (optional)

1 tablespoon sunflower oil

4 spring onions, chopped

2 tablespoons lime juice

To Serve:

hamburger buns

salad garnish

1 avocado, peeled, pitted, half diced and half thinly sliced

a few gherkins

tomato ketchup

½ onion, sliced into rings

Makes 6
Preparation time: 10 minutes
Cooking time: 10 minutes

the great steak sandwich

1 Heat 4 tablespoons of the olive oil in a medium frying pan. Add the mustard seeds, cover and let them pop for 30 seconds over a moderate heat – do not let them burn. Add the onions and garlic, cover and cook over a very low heat for 30 minutes, until very soft but not browned.

2 Process the softened onion mixture in a food processor or blender to a purée, then spoon into a bowl. Stir in the parsley and vinegar and season with salt and pepper to taste. Cover and set aside.

3 Brush the steaks with a little of the remaining oil. Season with pepper. Cook the steaks on the oiled grill of a preheated barbecue for about 5–6 minutes on each side.

4 Toast the bread slices on both sides until lightly golden. Spread each one with the onion purée. Slice the steaks thinly and divide between 4 of the bread slices. Top each one with the fontina, tomato slices and rocket. Season with salt and pepper to taste, top with the remaining bread slices and serve the steak sandwiches immediately.

6 tablespoons olive oil

2 teaspoons mustard seeds

2 large red onions, thinly sliced

2 garlic cloves, crushed

15 g (½ oz) flat leaf parsley, chopped

1 tablespoon balsamic vinegar

2 rump or sirloin steaks, about 250 g (8 oz) each

8 slices of olive bread or crusty bread

75 g (3 oz) fontina cheese, thinly sliced

2 ripe beefsteak tomatoes, sliced

125 g (4 oz) rocket

salt and pepper

Serves 4
Preparation time: 15 minutes
Cooking time: 40 minutes

1 Remove the skin from the chicken breasts and make 3 slashes into the flesh of each one.

2 Rub the chicken breasts with tandoori paste or powder and leave to marinate, preferably overnight but 30 minutes will be sufficient, if short of time.

3 Place the chicken breasts on the oiled grill of a preheated barbecue and cook for 8–10 minutes on each side, allowing a little charred colour to develop.

4 Meanwhile, heat the oil in a frying pan, add the onions and fry until slightly browned. Remove from the heat and stir in the chopped coriander. Serve the chicken with the onion and coriander mixture and garnish with lemon wedges and coriander sprigs.

4 boneless chicken breasts

4 tablespoons tandoori paste or tandoori powder

oil, for frying

2 onions, sliced

1 bunch coriander, chopped

To Garnish:

lemon wedges

coriander sprigs

Serves 4
Preparation time: 10 minutes, plus marinating
Cooking time: about 20 minutes

tandoori chicken

kofta
kebabs

1 To make the yogurt dip, mix the yogurt, chopped tomatoes and mint in a bowl. Season with a pinch of cayenne pepper and a pinch of salt. Cover the bowl and chill in the refrigerator until required.

2 Place the minced lamb or beef in a food processor or blender and blend to a smooth paste. Alternatively, pass through the finest blade of a mincer. Scrape into a bowl and stir in the onion, pine nuts, oregano, cumin and coriander. Season with salt and pepper to taste.

3 Mould the kebab mixture around 4 presoaked wooden or oiled metal skewers, forming it either into sausage shapes or balls. Cook the kebabs on the well-oiled grill of a preheated barbecue, turning them frequently, for about 10–12 minutes, until the meat is browned all over and cooked through.

4 Remove the kebabs from the skewers, if liked, or serve 1 skewer per person, with the yogurt dip and pitta bread and salad, if liked.

500 g (1 lb) minced lamb or beef

1 onion, grated

50 g (2 oz) pine nuts, roasted and chopped

1 tablespoon chopped fresh oregano

½ teaspoon ground cumin

½ teaspoon ground coriander

salt and pepper

To Serve: (optional)

pitta bread

salad

Yogurt Dip:

350 ml (12 fl oz) Greek yogurt

3 tomatoes, skinned, deseeded and chopped

1 tablespoon chopped mint

pinch of cayenne pepper

salt

Serves 4
Preparation time: 20 minutes
Cooking time: 10–12 minutes

barbecued pork with mustard dressing

1 Trim any excess fat from the pork. Mix together the ingredients for the mustard dressing in a bowl and add pepper to taste. Spread a thin layer over each pork chop and reserve the remainder.

2 Cook the chops on the oiled grill of a preheated barbecue for about 4 minutes on each side, spreading the second side with the mustard dressing when you turn them over.

3 Garnish the chops with lemon wedges and serve with a mixed green salad.

6 boneless pork loin chops

lemon wedges, to garnish

mixed green salad, to serve

Mustard Dressing:

3 tablespoons wholegrain mustard

4 tablespoons plain yogurt

pepper

Serves 6

Preparation time: 5 minutes

Cooking time: 8 minutes

homemade sausages with mustard aïoli

1 Soak the sausage casings in cold water for 20 minutes. Untangle any knots, then rinse by pulling one end of the casing over the end of the tap and running cold water through it.

2 Trim any skin or gristle from the pork shoulder and back fat and cut into pieces. Pass the meat through the medium blade of a mincer or finely chop it by hand. Place the meat in a large bowl and add the back fat, sea salt, thyme and bay and season with pepper. Mix well.

3 Spoon the sausagemeat into a large piping bag fitted with a large plain plastic nozzle. Wrinkle the open end of a sausage casing on to and up the nozzle and, holding the skin on to the nozzle, squeeze the filling into the casing to create a long sausage. Twist the sausage at intervals to make 8 large or 12 small sausages.

4 To make the mustard aïoli, place the garlic and egg yolks in a food processor or blender, add the lemon juice and process briefly to mix. With the motor running, gradually add the olive oil until the mixture forms a thick cream. Scrape the aïoli into a bowl, season with salt and pepper and stir in the mustard and more lemon juice if needed. Set aside.

5 Cook the sausages on the oiled grill of a preheated barbecue, turning often, for 10–15 minutes, until cooked through. Serve with the aïoli.

sausage casings

500 g (1 lb) lean shoulder pork

175 g (6 oz) back fat without rind

1½ tablespoons coarse sea salt

4 tablespoons thyme leaves

½ teaspoon ground bay leaf

pepper

Mustard Aïoli:

4–6 garlic cloves, crushed

2 egg yolks

juice of ½ lemon, plus extra to taste

300 ml (½ pint) extra virgin olive oil

2 tablespoons coarse grain mustard

salt and pepper

Serves 4
Preparation time: 1 hour
Cooking time: 10–15 minutes

tamarind spareribs with mint relish

1 To make the marinade, place the mustard seeds in a dry frying pan and cook over a low heat until the seeds start to pop. Remove the pan from the heat and leave the seeds to cool, then crush them lightly.

2 Mix the remaining marinade ingredients with the crushed mustard seeds. Place the spareribs in a large shallow dish and pour the marinade over. Turn the spareribs to coat, then cover and set aside to marinate for 1–2 hours.

3 To make the mint relish place the mint, onion, chilli, lemon juice and sugar in a food processor or blender. Process until smooth, pushing down with a spatula occasionally. Turn out into a bowl and season with salt and pepper to taste.

4 Remove the spareribs from the marinade and place on the oiled grill of a preheated barbecue and cook for 15–20 minutes, turning frequently. Serve the spareribs with the relish and a mixed salad.

1 kg (2 lb) meaty pork spareribs

mixed salad, to serve

Marinade:

1 teaspoon mustard seeds

3 tablespoons tamarind paste or 2 tablespoons lime or lemon juice

2 garlic cloves, crushed

1 tablespoon light soy sauce

6 tablespoons clear honey

1 teaspoon ground cumin

1 teaspoon ground coriander

½ teaspoon chilli powder

Mint Relish:

50 g (2 oz) chopped mint

½ small red onion, very finely chopped

1 small green chilli, deseeded and chopped

2 tablespoons lemon juice

1 teaspoon sugar

salt and pepper

Serves 4
Preparation time: 15 minutes, plus marinating
Cooking time: 15–20 minutes

turkey, tomato & tarragon burgers

1 Place the sun-dried tomatoes, turkey and tarragon in a food processor or blender and process until smooth. Spoon the mixture into a bowl and stir in the onion. Season with the paprika and salt. Mix well, divide into 4 and shape into burgers. Stretch 2 strips of pancetta over each burger and secure with cocktail sticks soaked in water for 30 minutes.

2 Cook the burgers on the oiled grill of a preheated barbecue for 20–25 minutes, turning frequently. Remove the cocktail sticks and serve immediately in the ciabatta rolls with shredded radicchio and lettuce.

8 sun-dried tomato halves in oil, drained and chopped

500 g (1 lb) minced turkey

1 tablespoon chopped tarragon

½ red onion, finely chopped

¼ teaspoon paprika

¼ teaspoon salt

4 slices smoked pancetta or rindless streaky bacon, cut in half

To Serve:

4 ciabatta rolls

shredded radicchio and Cos lettuce

Serves 4	
Preparation time: 20 minutes	
Cooking time: 20–25 minutes	

winchester sausages

1 Mix the pork and pork fat together in a bowl. Pour the milk over the breadcrumbs and set aside for 10 minutes. Squeeze the bread-crumbs dry and add to the meat. Add the garlic, spices, herbs and salt and pepper to taste and mix well.

2 Using a piping bag fitted with a large plain nozzle, carefully force the sausage mixture into the casings. Push the mixture evenly along the casing then twist to form sausages.

3 Cook on the oiled grill of a preheated barbecue, turning frequently, for 15–20 minutes, until golden brown and thoroughly cooked. Garnish with thyme sprigs.

■ If you thread sausages on to skewers before placing them on the grill, they are easier to turn.

250 g (8 oz) belly pork, minced

250 g (8 oz) lean minced pork

25 g (1 oz) pork fat, minced

6 tablespoons milk

75 g (3 oz) wholemeal breadcrumbs

1 garlic clove, crushed

¼ teaspoon ground mace

¼ teaspoon ground allspice

1 tablespoon chopped parsley

1 tablespoon chopped sage

1 teaspoon chopped thyme, extra, sprigs, to garnish

salt and pepper

1 metre (1 yard) sausage casing

Makes about 10–12

Preparation time: 25 minutes

Cooking time: 15–20 minutes

duck with olives & oranges

1 Place one duck breast, skin side up, on a doubled piece of foil, sprinkle with half of the salt and top with a second duck breast, skin side down. Wrap in foil. Repeat with the remaining pair of duck breasts. Chill both parcels for at least 12 hours.

2 Finely grate the rind of 2 of the oranges, then peel and segment all 4 over a bowl to catch any juices. Place the segments in the bowl and mix in the ginger and olives. Place this mixture on a doubled piece of foil with the edges turned up and dot with the butter. Place the parcel on the oiled grill of a preheated barbecue for 25–30 minutes.

3 Meanwhile, separate the duck breasts, rinse them and pat dry on kitchen paper. Cook on the oiled barbecue grill, skin side down for 5 minutes, then turn and seal the other side. Cook the duck alongside the parcel of olives and oranges for 10–15 minutes, turning once, until the duck skin is crisp and the flesh tender but still pink. Serve with the olive and orange mixture and a leafy salad.

4 duck breast fillets, about 250 g (8 oz) each

4 oranges

2 pieces of stem ginger in syrup, drained and chopped

125 g (4 oz) black olives

15 g (½ oz) butter

leafy salad, to serve

Serves 4

Preparation time: 15 minutes, plus chilling

Cooking time: 25–30 minutes

south-east asian grilled chicken with pineapple & peanut relish

1 Cut 3 diagonal slits in each chicken breast. Place the chicken in a shallow dish large enough to hold all the breasts in a single layer. Place all the ingredients for the marinade in a blender or food processor and process until smooth. Pour over the chicken, cover and set aside to marinate for 1–1¼ hours.

2 Meanwhile, make the relish. Mix together all the ingredients in a bowl, cover and set aside.

3 Remove the chicken breasts from the marinade and reserve the marinade. Cook the chicken on the oiled grill of a preheated barbecue, turning and brushing often with the reserved marinade, for 25–30 minutes, or until cooked through.

4 Transfer to individual plates and serve with the peanut and pineapple relish and steamed rice, if liked. Garnish with lime halves.

4 part-boned chicken breasts

steamed rice, to serve (optional)

Marinade:

2 sticks lemon grass, finely chopped

juice of 2 limes

2 red chillies, deseeded and chopped

3 garlic cloves, crushed

2.5 cm (1 inch) piece of fresh root ginger, finely chopped

2 tablespoons soft dark brown sugar

2 tablespoons chopped coriander

150 ml (¼ pint) coconut milk

Relish:

1 small pineapple, peeled, cored and finely chopped

1 red onion, chopped

3 tablespoons freshly squeezed lime juice

1 garlic clove, crushed

1 tablespoon light soy sauce

25 g (1 oz) roasted unsalted peanuts, chopped

Serves 4

Preparation time: 30 minutes, plus marinating

Cooking time: 25–30 minutes

seafood kebabs •

fish steaks with mint pesto •

red snapper & spicy salsa •

swordfish with black olive butter •

rainbow trout with herb stuffing •

barbecued trout with garlic & rosemary •

cajun-style cod •

spicy fish satay •

prawn & chicken kebabs •

grilled sardines with chilli oil •

spiedini of prawns in a balsamic marinade •

salmon steaks with teriyaki sauce •

barbecued tuna with shallot jus •

fish & shellfish

seafood kebabs

1 Cut the plaice into chunks and cut the sardines in half.

2 Mix together the marinade ingredients in a large bowl, with salt and pepper to taste, add all the fish and shellfish and mix well. Leave to marinate for 30 minutes, stirring occasionally.

3 Remove the fish from the marinade and reserve any marinade. Cut the bacon rashers in half and roll up. Arrange the fish alternately on to 4 presoaked wooden or oiled metal skewers with the bacon, interspersing with bay leaves and lemon wedges to taste.

4 Place the kebabs on the oiled grill of a preheated barbecue for 5–7 minutes on each side, basting with the marinade.

250 g (8 oz) plaice fillets

4 sardines or other small fish

8 large cooked unshelled prawns

4 scallops, halved

8 rashers streaky bacon, derinded

8 bay leaves

2 lemons, cut into wedges

Marinade:

juice of 1 lemon

4 tablespoons olive oil

1 bouquet garni

salt and pepper

Serves 4

Preparation time: 15 minutes, plus marinating

Cooking time: 10–14 minutes

4 halibut or cod steaks, about
175 g (6 oz) each

olive oil, for brushing

2–3 tablespoons lemon juice

salt and pepper

shredded lettuce, to serve (optional)

1 First, make the mint pesto. Place all the ingredients in a food processor or blender and process until fairly smooth. Season with salt and pepper to taste and transfer to a bowl.

2 Brush the fish steaks with olive oil and sprinkle over the lemon juice. Season with salt and pepper and cook the fish on the oiled grill of a preheated barbecue for about 3–4 minutes on each side, until golden and cooked through.

3 Serve the fish steaks on a bed of shredded lettuce, if liked, spread with a spoonful of the pesto.

Mint Pesto:

6 tablespoons chopped mint

1 tablespoon chopped parsley

1 garlic clove, chopped

1 tablespoon freshly grated
Parmesan cheese

1 tablespoon double cream

1 teaspoon balsamic vinegar

3 tablespoons extra virgin olive oil

Serves 4
Preparation time: 10 minutes
Cooking time: 6–8 minutes

fish steaks with mint pesto

red snapper & spicy salsa

1 Combine all the salsa ingredients, cover and set aside to marinate for 2–3 hours if possible. If you prefer a smooth salsa, place all the ingredients in a food processor or blender and process.

2 Place the snapper fillets, skin side down, on the oiled grill of a preheated barbecue and cook for 3–4 minutes. Turn over and cook for a further 3 minutes, or until firm to the touch. Serve with the spicy salsa and garnish with sprigs of coriander.

■ There are several different kinds of snapper, ranging in colour from blue-green to red, orange and pink. They are sub-tropical fish with a fine, rich flavour. If snapper is not available, use red mullet instead.

4 x 175 g (6 oz) red snapper fillets

coriander sprigs, to garnish

Spicy Salsa:

6 tomatoes, skinned, deseeded and chopped

1 bunch of spring onions, chopped

1 garlic clove, crushed

1 bunch of coriander, chopped

2 chillies, deseeded and diced

juice of 2 limes

1 ripe avocado, peeled, stoned and diced

2 tablespoons olive oil

salt and pepper

Serves 4
Preparation time: 20 minutes, plus marinating
Cooking time: 6–8 minutes

swordfish with black olive butter

1 To make the black olive butter, place the butter in a bowl and add the olives, anchovy paste, garlic, capers and lemon juice and rind. Beat until well combined and season with salt and pepper to taste.

2 Place a piece of greaseproof paper on a work surface and spread the butter down the middle. Roll the paper over and twist the ends until you have a neat sausage. Chill in the refrigerator until firm.

3 Brush the swordfish steaks with the olive oil, place on the oiled grill of a preheated barbecue and grill for 3–4 minutes on each side until just cooked. Unroll the black olive butter and cut into slices. Serve each steak with a slice of butter on top.

4 swordfish steaks, about 175 g (6 oz) each

2 tablespoons olive oil

Black Olive Butter:

125 g (4 oz) unsalted butter, softened

25 g (1 oz) pitted black olives, very finely chopped

½ teaspoon anchovy paste

1 garlic clove, crushed

1 tablespoon capers, finely chopped

juice and finely grated rind of ½ lemon

salt and pepper

Serves 4

Preparation time: 10 minutes, plus marinating

Cooking time: 10–15 minutes

■ Swordfish is increasingly available and has a firm, meaty texture. Make sure you brush it well with oil before grilling as the flesh dries out easily.

rainbow trout
with herb stuffing

1 Mix together the lime juice, herbs, shallot, butter and salt and pepper to taste. Divide the mixture into 4 portions and spread in the cavities of the trout. Secure with cocktail sticks or sew up.

2 Wrap a rasher of bacon around each trout. Place each fish on a piece of foil, top with a lime slice and a rosemary sprig and seal the foil securely. Cook on the oiled grill of a preheated barbecue for 10 minutes each side. Serve in the foil.

2 tablespoons lime juice

1 tablespoon chopped parsley

1 tablespoon chopped thyme

1 tablespoon snipped chives

1 shallot, very finely chopped

25 g (1 oz) butter, softened

4 rainbow trout, cleaned

4 rashers streaky bacon, derinded

4 lime slices

4 rosemary sprigs

salt and pepper

Serves 4

Preparation time: 15 minutes

Cooking time: 20 minutes

barbecued trout with garlic & rosemary

1 Mix together the garlic and rosemary and use to fill the body cavity of each trout. Place the fish in a shallow dish. Mix the olive oil with salt and pepper to taste and the lemon rind and juice. Spoon this mixture evenly over the trout. Cover the fish and chill for 3–4 hours.

2 Remove the trout from the marinade and reserve any marinade. Place the fish on the oiled grill of a preheated barbecue and cook for 6 minutes.

3 Brush the trout on both sides with the marinade, and then grill on the second side for a further 6 minutes, or until they are tender.

4 Meanwhile, press an almond into each green olive, then roll the olives lightly in the remaining marinade.

5 Arrange the cooked trout on a serving dish, garnish with the almond-stuffed olives, lemon slices, rosemary sprigs and serve with a green salad.

2 garlic cloves, crushed

2 rosemary sprigs, divided into short lengths, extra, to garnish

4 trout, about 175–250 g (6–8 oz) each

6 tablespoons olive oil

finely grated rind of ½ lemon

3 tablespoons lemon juice

salt and pepper

green salad, to serve

To Garnish:

16 blanched almonds

16 pitted green olives

lemon slices

Serves 4

Preparation time: 10 minutes, plus marinating

Cooking time: about 12 minutes

cajun-style cod

1 To make the guacamole, cut the avocado in half and remove the stone. Scoop the flesh into a food processor or blender, add the lime juice and process until smooth. Spoon the avocado mixture into a bowl and stir in the chopped tomato, coriander and onion. Season with salt and pepper to taste. Cover tightly and set aside.

2 Place the garlic, salt and all the herbs and spices in a mortar and grind with a pestle until smooth. Tip the mixture into a shallow dish and stir in the flour.

3 Pour the melted butter into a second shallow dish. Dip the fish fillets into the melted butter, then dust with the spiced flour. Place the fish on the oiled grill of a preheated barbecue and cook for about 2–3 minutes on each side.

4 Meanwhile, cut the unpeeled plantains in half lengthways, if using, and brush with the lime juice. Place on the barbecue grill, skin side down. Cook for 2 minutes, until the skin is well blackened, then turn and grill for 1 minute more, or until the flesh is just cooked.

5 Serve the Cajun fish with the guacamole, grilled plantains and garnish with lime wedges. Add a crisp green salad, if liked.

4 garlic cloves, crushed

1 teaspoon salt

2 tablespoons chopped oregano

2 tablespoons chopped thyme

1 teaspoon cumin seeds

1–2 teaspoons chilli powder

4 green cardamom pods, seeds removed

12 allspice berries

2 teaspoons mixed peppercorns

2 teaspoons paprika

25 g (1 oz) plain flour

125 g (4 oz) butter, melted

4 cod fillets, about 200–250 g (7–8 oz) each

2 ripe plantains (optional)

juice of ½ lime

lime wedges, to garnish

green salad, to serve (optional)

Guacamole:

1 large avocado

juice of 1 lime

1 large tomato, skinned, deseeded and chopped

1 tablespoon chopped coriander

1 small onion, finely chopped

salt and pepper

Serves 4
Preparation time: 20 minutes
Cooking time: 4–6 minutes

spicy fish satay

1 Cut each mackerel fillet into 2.5 cm (1 inch) diagonal strips and place in a bowl. Mix together the garlic, ginger, soy sauce, lime or lemon juice and chilli and pour over the mackerel. Turn to coat well, cover and set aside to marinate for 30 minutes–1 hour.

2 To make the satay sauce, heat the oil in a small saucepan. Add the garlic and shallot and cook for 3–4 minutes, until lightly golden. Add the water, sugar, chilli powder and peanuts, stir well and bring to the boil. Reduce the heat and simmer, stirring occasionally, for 10–15 minutes, or until the sauce has thickened. Remove from the heat and stir in the lime or lemon juice and season with salt and pepper to taste. Keep warm on the side of the barbecue.

3 Remove the fish from the marinade and thread 3 pieces on to each of 4 presoaked wooden or oiled metal skewers, adding a piece of papaya to the end of each one.

4 Place the skewers on the oiled grill of a preheated barbecue and cook for 3–4 minutes on each side. Serve with the warm satay sauce.

500 g (1 lb) mackerel fillets

1 garlic clove, crushed

2.5 cm (1 inch) piece of fresh root ginger, chopped and crushed in a garlic press

2 teaspoons light soy sauce

1 tablespoon lime or lemon juice

1 small red chilli, very finely chopped

½ papaya, peeled, deseeded and cut into chunks

Satay Sauce:

2 tablespoons sunflower or groundnut oil

1 large garlic clove, crushed

1 shallot, finely chopped

400 ml (14 fl oz) water

1 tablespoon dark brown sugar

½ teaspoon chilli powder

125 g (4 oz) unsalted roasted peanuts, finely ground

1 tablespoon lime or lemon juice

salt and pepper

Serves 4

Preparation time: 30 minutes, plus marinating

Cooking time: 20–25 minutes

1 Thread the prawns, chicken and pepper squares alternately on to presoaked wooden or oiled metal skewers.

2 Place the skewers in a shallow dish and pour the marinade over. Turn the skewers to coat with the marinade. Cover and set aside to marinate for 2 hours in a cool place, turning occasionally.

3 Remove the kebabs from the marinade and reserve any marinade. Cook the kebabs on the oiled grill of a preheated barbecue for about 20 minutes, turning and basting frequently with the reserved marinade.

4 Garnish the kebabs with sprigs of mint and serve with lime wedges.

20 cooked Mediterranean or large prawns, thawed if frozen

750 g (1½ lb) boneless, skinless chicken breast, cut into 2.5 cm (1 inch) cubes

1 small yellow or red pepper, cored, deseeded and cut into 2.5 cm (1 inch) squares

1 small green pepper, cored, deseeded and cut into 2.5 cm (1 inch) squares

1 quantity Herb Marinade (see page 81)

mint sprigs, to garnish

lime wedges, to serve

Serves 6–8

Preparation time: 15 minutes, plus marinating

Cooking time: about 20 minutes

prawn & chicken kebabs

125 ml (4 fl oz) olive oil

2 tablespoons chopped dried red chillies

12 small sardines, cleaned and scaled

coarse sea salt

To Serve:

lemon wedges

crusty bread

tomato and onion salad (optional)

Serves 4

Preparation time: 15 minutes, plus infusing

Cooking time: 6–8 minutes

---

1 Place the oil and chillies in a small saucepan. Heat very gently for about 10 minutes. Remove from the heat, cover and leave to cool and infuse for 8–12 hours or overnight.

2 Strain the chilli oil through a sieve lined with muslin or a clean tea towel. Pour into a sterilized jar or bottle.

3 Brush the sardines with a little of the chilli oil, sprinkle with coarse sea salt and cook on the oiled grill of a preheated barbecue for 6–8 minutes, or until just cooked, turning once. Serve immediately, with lemon wedges, crusty bread and a tomato and onion salad, if liked.

grilled sardines with chilli oil

■ The easiest way to scale sardines is to run your hand along the length of the fish, from tail to head, two or three times. This is best done under cold running water.

spiedini of prawns in a balsamic marinade

1 To prepare the prawns, remove the legs and cut off the heads with a small sharp knife. Holding a prawn with the back uppermost, slice along its length, from the thickest part towards the tail, cutting almost but not quite through it. Carefully remove the dark vein that runs down its back. Gently press the prawn to flatten it and make a butterfly shape. Repeat with the remaining prawns then rinse well under running water. Pat the prawns dry on kitchen paper and place them in a large shallow dish.

2 Mix together the oil, vinegar, oregano or marjoram, garlic and pepper and pour over the prawns, turning to coat them well. Cover and set aside to marinate for 1 hour.

3 Remove the prawns from the marinade and reserve any marinade. Thread 3 prawns on to each of 4 presoaked wooden or oiled metal skewers.

4 Cook the prawns on the oiled grill of a preheated barbecue for 3–4 minutes, turning them once and basting with any remaining marinade, until the flesh is opaque and just cooked. Serve immediately.

12 large raw king prawns in their shells

5 tablespoons olive oil

2 tablespoons balsamic vinegar

2 tablespoons chopped oregano or marjoram

2 garlic cloves, crushed

pepper

Serves 4

Preparation time: 20 minutes, plus marinating

Cooking time: 3–4 minutes

■ Take care not to overcook the prawns or they will become tough.

salmon steaks with teriyaki sauce

1 To make the sauce, place all the ingredients in a small saucepan and bring to the boil. Simmer rapidly for 10 minutes or until reduced to a thick, glossy sauce. Allow to cool for 5 minutes before using as it will be extremely hot.

2 Cook the salmon steaks on the oiled grill of a preheated barbecue for 4 minutes on each side, until charred and firm to the touch.

3 Arrange the pieces of lettuce on 4 plates. Place the salmon steaks on top of the lettuce. Spoon the sauce over the salmon and let it run over the lettuce. Serve immediately.

4 x 175 g (6 oz) salmon steaks

4 little gem lettuces, quartered lengthways

Teriyaki Sauce:

1 tablespoon sunflower oil

1 tablespoon sesame oil

6 tablespoons teriyaki marinade

2 tablespoons rice or white wine vinegar

juice of 1 lime

2 tablespoons clear honey

Serves 4

Preparation time: 15 minutes

Cooking time: about 20 minutes

■ Teriyaki sauce is available bottled from most supermarkets and speciality food shops.

barbecued tuna with shallot jus

1 First, make the shallot jus. Mix the shallots, red wine and Marsala in a saucepan, season with salt and pepper and bring to the boil. Boil rapidly until reduced by half. Keep warm on the side of the barbecue.

2 Cook the tuna steaks on the oiled grill of a preheated barbecue for 3 minutes on each side.

3 Pour the sauce over the tuna steaks and serve garnished with parsley sprigs and with a spoonful of mashed potato, if liked.

4 tuna steaks, about 100 g (3½ oz) each

flat leaf parsley sprigs, to garnish

mashed potato, to serve (optional)

Shallot Jus:

4 shallots, finely chopped

300 ml (½ pint) red wine

150 ml (¼ pint) Marsala

salt and pepper

Serves 4
Preparation time: 5 minutes
Cooking time: about 15 minutes

red chilli polenta chips & grilled garlic skewers •

red bean & rice patties •

mixed pepper kebabs •

sweet potato & chilli salad •

stuffed courgettes •

buttered corn on the cob •

grilled sweet potatoes & aïoli •

stuffed mini peppers with tomato sauce •

garlic potatoes baked in foil •

baby aubergines with herbed greek yogurt •

vegetarian
dishes

red chilli polenta chips & grilled garlic skewers

1 Bring the measured water and salt to the boil in a large saucepan. Reduce the heat slightly and add the polenta in a thin stream, beating constantly. Cook, stirring constantly, for 20–30 minutes, until the mixture comes away from the sides of the pan.

2 Immediately stir in the Parmesan, sun-dried tomatoes and chopped red chillies. Tip the polenta out on to a board or baking sheet. Leave to cool, then cut into chunky chips.

3 Meanwhile, bring a small pan of water to the boil and add the garlic cloves. Reduce the heat and simmer for 10 minutes. Drain. When cool enough to handle, skewer 3 garlic cloves on to each of 4 presoaked wooden cocktail sticks.

4 Brush the polenta chips and garlic skewers with the oil and cook on the oiled grill of a preheated barbecue for about 3 minutes on each side, until the garlic is soft and the polenta is charred and golden.

750 ml (1¼ pints) water

1 teaspoon salt

250 g (8 oz) polenta

50 g (2 oz) Parmesan cheese, finely grated

8 sun-dried tomato halves in oil, drained and finely chopped

4 large red chillies, grilled, peeled, deseeded and finely chopped

12 garlic cloves, unpeeled

6 tablespoons olive oil

Serves 4
Preparation time: 10 minutes
Cooking time: 30–35 minutes

■ These polenta chips are ideal snacks to serve to guests with a drink, while you are cooking the main dishes.

red bean & rice patties

1 Place the beans in a colander. Rinse under cold running water and drain well, then mash.

2 Bring a saucepan of salted water to the boil. Add the rice, lower the heat and simmer for 20 minutes, or until just cooked, or according to packet instructions. Drain, rinse under cold running water, and drain well.

3 Heat the oil in a frying pan, add the onion, garlic and chilli and cook for 5 minutes. Add the cumin seeds, coriander and turmeric and cook for 1–2 minutes, then add the onion mixture to the mashed beans. Stir in the rice and mix. Add the eggs and salt and pepper to taste, then mix.

4 To make the sauce, place the coriander, pistachios and chillies in a food processor or blender and process until smooth. Scrape the mixture into a bowl, stir in the yogurt and season with salt and pepper to taste.

5 Divide the bean and rice mixture into 4 portions and shape into rounds. Brush them with oil, then place on the oiled grill of a preheated barbecue and cook for 4–5 minutes on each side, until a crust has formed. Garnish the patties with lime wedges and serve with the sauce.

125 g (4 oz) canned red kidney beans

125 g (4 oz) brown rice

1 tablespoon groundnut oil

1 onion, finely chopped

1 garlic clove, crushed

1 green chilli, deseeded and finely chopped

1 teaspoon cumin seeds

1 teaspoon ground coriander

½ teaspoon turmeric

2 eggs, beaten

salt and pepper

lime wedges, to garnish

Sauce:

3 tablespoons chopped coriander

25 g (1 oz) pistachio nuts, chopped

2 green chillies, deseeded and finely chopped

125 ml (4 fl oz) Greek yogurt

Serves 4
Preparation time: 15 minutes
Cooking time: 35–40 minutes

mixed pepper kebabs

1 Thread the pepper squares alternately on to presoaked wooden or oiled metal skewers. Brush the peppers generously on all sides with the oil and cook on the oiled grill of a preheated barbecue for 7–10 minutes, turning and brushing with oil every 1–2 minutes. When they are just beginning to char, they are done. Brush again with the oil.

2 Place the skewers on warmed serving plates, then sprinkle each one with a little of the chopped garlic. Season generously with salt and crushed peppercorns then pour over some lemon juice. Serve immediately with crusty bread and a green salad.

2 large green peppers, cored, deseeded and cut into 2.5 cm (1 inch) squares

2 large red peppers, cored, deseeded and cut into 2.5 cm (1 inch) squares

2 large yellow peppers, cored, deseeded and cut into 2.5 cm (1 inch) squares

about 125 ml (4 fl oz) olive oil

2 garlic cloves, finely chopped

coarsely ground sea salt

1 tablespoon black peppercorns, lightly crushed

3 tablespoons lemon juice

crusty bread and green salad, to serve

| **Serves 4–6** |
| **Preparation time**: 10 minutes |
| **Cooking time**: 7–10 minutes |

sweet potato & chilli salad

1 Cook the sweet potato slices in a large pan of boiling water for about 5 minutes. Drain well and then refresh under cold running water. Spread on kitchen paper to dry.

2 To make the dressing, mix together all the ingredients in a small bowl until blended or shake together in a screw-top jar. Set aside.

3 Cook the chillies on the oiled grill of a preheated barbecue, turning frequently, until the skins are blistered and blackened all over. Allow them to cool slightly, then carefully remove and discard the skin and seeds. Cut the flesh into thin strips and set aside.

4 Brush the sweet potato slices with the groundnut oil. Arrange the sweet potato slices on the barbecue grill and cook until crisp and lightly browned. Alternatively, cook under a preheated moderate grill. Transfer to a large serving bowl when done and add more to the grill.

5 Add the chilli strips and coriander to the bowl. Season with coarse sea salt and pepper to taste. Toss lightly to mix. Just before serving, pour the dressing over and toss well. Serve with the lettuce or rocket.

750 g (1½ lb) sweet potatoes, peeled and sliced

3 large red chillies

6 tablespoons groundnut oil

25 g (1 oz) coriander leaves, torn

salt and pepper

lettuce leaves or rocket, to serve

Dressing:

1 teaspoon finely grated lime rind

2 tablespoons lime juice

4 tablespoons peanut oil

2 tablespoons sesame oil

Serves 4
Preparation time: 15 minutes
Cooking time: about 20 minutes

■ When buying sweet potatoes, make sure that they are really firm and don't have any bruises on them.

stuffed courgettes

1 Plunge the courgettes into a saucepan of salted boiling water. Cook until just tender, then drain and refresh under cold running water for a few minutes to set the colour. Split the courgettes lengthways, scoop out the centres and discard.

2 To make the filling, melt the butter in a frying pan and add the onion and red pepper. Cook gently, for about 5 minutes, until soft. Add the peas to the pan.

3 In a bowl, beat the dill, cream, salt and pepper with the eggs, and pour into the pan of vegetables. Stir gently until the eggs are lightly scrambled in the vegetable mixture. Remove from the heat.

4 Fill the halved courgettes with the egg and vegetable mixture. Carefully place the courgettes on the oiled grill of a preheated barbecue for 1–2 minutes to heat through. Arrange the courgettes on a serving dish and serve immediately.

6 courgettes, about 12 cm (5 inches) in length, topped and tailed

50 g (2 oz) butter

1 onion, finely chopped

1 red pepper, cored, deseeded and finely chopped

75 g (3 oz) frozen peas, blanched

1 teaspoon dried dill

2 tablespoons single cream

4 eggs, beaten

salt and pepper

Serves 6

Preparation time: 15 minutes

Cooking time: about 25 minutes

1 Cook the corn cobs in salted boiling water for 7 minutes.

2 Meanwhile, make the herb butter. Mix together the softened butter, lemon juice, parsley, thyme and chives and salt and pepper to taste.

3 Drain the corn cobs and place each one on individual double-thickness pieces of foil. Place a quarter of the herb butter on each corn cob and wrap up the foil to secure tightly, ensuring that there is nowhere for the butter to escape.

4 Cook the cobs on the oiled grill of a preheated barbecue for about 20–25 minutes, until the corn is tender. Serve immediately.

4 corn cobs

Herb Butter:
125 g (4 oz) butter, softened
1 teaspoon lemon juice
1 tablespoon chopped parsley
1 tablespoon chopped thyme
1 tablespoon snipped chives
salt and pepper

Serves 4

Preparation time: 5 minutes

Cooking time: about 30 minutes

buttered corn on the cob

1 To make the aïoli, place the garlic and egg yolks in a food processor or blender, add the lemon juice and process briefly to mix. With the motor running, gradually add the olive oil in a thin steady stream until the mixture forms a thick cream. Season with salt and pepper to taste and stir in more lemon juice, if liked. Scrape the aïoli into a bowl and set aside.

2 To prepare the sweet potatoes, cut each potato into 5 mm (¼ inch) slices, brush with the olive oil and place them on the oiled grill of a preheated barbecue. Grill for about 5 minutes on each side, until tender. Serve hot with the aïoli.

500 g (1 lb) sweet potatoes, scrubbed

4 tablespoons olive oil

salt and pepper

Aïoli:

4–6 garlic cloves, crushed

2 egg yolks

juice of ½ lemon, plus extra, to taste

300 ml (½ pint) extra virgin olive oil

Serves 4
Preparation time: 15 minutes
Cooking time: 10 minutes

grilled sweet potatoes & aïoli

stuffed mini peppers with tomato sauce

1 To make the sauce, heat the oil in a saucepan. Add the onion and the garlic and cook for 5 minutes, until softened but not brown. Stir in the canned tomatoes, parsley and oregano and simmer for 10 minutes. Strain the sauce through a sieve set over a clean pan. Set aside.

2 To make the stuffing, combine the goats' cheese, ricotta and mint in a bowl. Stir in the chilli, if using, and season with salt and pepper to taste.

3 Make a small slit in the side of each pepper and carefully scrape out the seeds and core with a teaspoon, keeping the pepper shells intact. Half fill each pepper with stuffing – do not be tempted to fill them completely, or they may burst during cooking.

4 Cook the filled peppers on the oiled grill of a preheated barbecue for about 10–15 minutes, turning occasionally, until softened. Meanwhile, reheat the tomato sauce by placing the pan at the edge of the barbecue grill.

5 Place 2 of the filled peppers on each plate and serve with the tomato sauce and a generous spoonful of Greek yogurt.

8 mini peppers

Greek yogurt, to serve

Tomato Sauce:

1 tablespoon olive oil

1 onion, finely chopped

1 garlic clove, crushed

400 g (13 oz) can tomatoes

1 tablespoon chopped parsley

1 tablespoon chopped oregano

Stuffing:

125 g (4 oz) soft fresh goats' cheese

50 g (2 oz) ricotta cheese

1½ tablespoons chopped mint

1 red or green chilli, deseeded and finely chopped (optional)

salt and pepper

Serves 4
Preparation time: 20 minutes
Cooking time: 10–15 minutes

garlic potatoes baked in foil

1 Cream together the butter, garlic and chives and season with salt and pepper to taste.

2 Blanch the potatoes in salted boiling water for 2–3 minutes. Drain and place on 4 individual doubled pieces of foil. Turn the edges of the foil towards the centre, place a quarter of the garlic butter in each foil package. Secure the foil tightly to ensure that no butter escapes. Place in the coals of a preheated barbecue and cook for 30–45 minutes, until the potatoes are tender. Transfer them to a serving dish.

75 g (3 oz) butter, softened

2 garlic cloves, crushed

2 tablespoons snipped chives

750 g (1½ lb) new potatoes, scrubbed

salt and pepper

Serves 4
Preparation time: 10 minutes
Cooking time: 30–45 minutes

baby aubergines with herbed greek yogurt

1 To make the herbed Greek yogurt, mix all the ingredients together in a bowl and set aside.

2 Slice the baby aubergines in half lengthways, leaving the stalks attached. Using a small brush, coat the aubergines with the olive oil. Cook them on the oiled grill of a preheated barbecue for about 2–3 minutes on each side.

3 To serve, place the aubergines on a serving dish or plate and spoon over the herbed yogurt.

■ There are now many baby vegetables available in supermarkets. They are ideal for starters or side dishes.

12 baby aubergines

3 tablespoons olive oil

salt and pepper

Herbed Greek Yogurt:

2 tablespoons chopped parsley

2 tablespoons chopped dill

2 tablespoons chopped mint

1 small red onion, finely chopped

2 garlic cloves, crushed

75 g (3 oz) Kalamata or large black olives, pitted and sliced

2 teaspoons fennel seeds, crushed

1 tablespoon capers, chopped

15 g (½ oz) gherkins, finely chopped

finely grated rind and juice of 1 lime

150 ml (¼ pint) Greek yogurt

salt and pepper

Serves 4

Preparation time: 20 minutes

Cooking time: 4–6 minutes

pepper & chickpea salad with orange dressing ●

spinach, bacon, avocado & mushroom salad ●

warm sweet potato & walnut salad ●

tarragon & thyme chicken salad ●

summer garden salad ●

mushroom & butter bean salad ●

cucumber & dill salad ●

tuscan salad ●

braised mediterranean vegetables ●

spiced okra ●

fresh mayonnaise ●

basic barbecue sauce ●

herb marinade ●

salads &
side dishes

pepper & chickpea salad with orange dressing

1 Cook the chickpeas in unsalted boiling water for 1–2 hours, or until they are tender.

2 Meanwhile, place the peppers on the oiled grill of a preheated barbecue for 15 minutes, turning them frequently, until the skins blacken and blister. Hold the peppers under cold water then, using a small sharp knife, peel off the skins. Cut the peppers in half, discard the cores and seeds, and slice the flesh into thin strips.

3 To make the orange dressing, mix together the orange rind and juice, the sunflower oil and garlic in a large bowl. Season with salt and pepper to taste.

4 Drain the chickpeas and toss in the orange dressing while they are still hot. Set aside to cool.

5 Stir in the red peppers and coriander. Turn the salad into a serving dish.

200 g (7 oz) dried chickpeas, soaked overnight and drained

2 red peppers

2 yellow peppers

2 tablespoons chopped coriander

Orange Dressing:

½ teaspoon grated orange rind

2 tablespoons orange juice

3 tablespoons sunflower oil

1 garlic clove, crushed

salt and pepper

Serves 4

Preparation time: 10 minutes, plus soaking

Cooking time: 1–2 hours

spinach, bacon, avocado & mushroom salad

1 To make the dressing, place all the ingredients in a screw-top jar with salt and pepper and shake well.

2 Grill the bacon until crisp. Drain on kitchen paper and chop into bite-sized pieces. Line a large salad bowl with the spinach and then add the bacon and mushrooms.

3 Slice the avocados thinly and spoon over the lemon juice. Add them to the salad bowl. Pour over the dressing and toss lightly. Garnish with herb sprigs and serve.

175 g (6 oz) rindless smoked bacon

250 g (8 oz) young spinach leaves, stalks removed and shredded

75 g (3 oz) chestnut or button mushrooms, thinly sliced

2 small avocados, peeled, halved and stoned

2 tablespoons lemon juice

herb sprigs, to garnish

Dressing:

175 ml (6 fl oz) extra virgin olive oil

75 ml (3 fl oz) cider vinegar

2 tablespoons chopped mixed herbs

1 teaspoon clear honey

1 garlic clove, crushed

pinch of mustard powder

salt and pepper

Serves 4

Preparation time: 10 minutes

Cooking time: 8–10 minutes

■ If they are available, you could use 6 baby avocados, peeled and thinly sliced.

warm sweet potato
& walnut salad

1 Peel the sweet potatoes, cut
them in half lengthways, then cut
across into 1 cm (½ inch) slices.

2 Bring a saucepan of lightly salted
water to the boil, add the sweet
potatoes and cook for 5 minutes, until
just tender. Drain well.

3 Mix together the walnut oil,
vinegar, shallot and garlic in
a large bowl. Add the warm sweet
potatoes, walnuts and raisins and toss
well. Add salt and pepper to taste and
serve warm or chilled.

500 g (1 lb) sweet potatoes

5 tablespoons walnut oil

1 tablespoon white wine vinegar

1 shallot, finely chopped

1 garlic clove, crushed

50 g (2 oz) walnuts, chopped

50 g (2 oz) seedless raisins

salt and pepper

Serves 4
Preparation time: 15 minutes
Cooking time: 5 minutes

tarragon & thyme chicken salad

1 Remove and discard the skin from the cold roast chicken and chop the meat into bite-sized pieces. Place it in a bowl with the celery, apple and green pepper.

2 To make the dressing, mix the mayonnaise with the soured cream, mustard and salt and pepper to taste. Fold into the chicken mixture to coat evenly.

3 Line individual serving plates with the lettuce leaves and top with the chicken mixture. Sprinkle with the toasted almonds and garnish with tarragon and celery leaves. Serve immediately or lightly chilled.

2 kg (4 lb) chicken, roasted

4 celery sticks, sliced

1 red dessert apple, cored and chopped

1 green pepper, cored, deseeded and chopped

½ round lettuce, separated into leaves

25 g (1 oz) slivered almonds, toasted

Dressing:

4 tablespoons mayonnaise

4 tablespoons soured cream

2 tablespoons tarragon and thyme mustard

salt and pepper

To Garnish:

tarragon leaves

celery leaves

Serves 4–6

Preparation time: 15 minutes

summer garden salad

1 Bring a saucepan of water to the boil. Add the cauliflower florets. When the water returns to the boil, cook the florets for about 3 minutes, until just tender. Drain in a colander and refresh under cold running water, then drain again thoroughly.

2 Add the peas to a saucepan of boiling water. Cook for 4 minutes then drain, refresh and cool as for the cauliflower.

3 Combine the cauliflower, peas, radishes and spring onions in a serving bowl. Add the parsley together with salt and pepper to taste.

4 To make the dressing, stir all the ingredients together in a small bowl. Adjust the seasoning to taste. Drizzle over the salad and toss lightly. To serve, garnish with mint sprigs.

■ There are a number of different kinds of mint, some of which, such as lemon and apple mint, have undertones of other flavours. Try experimenting with these, pineapple or Bowles mint.

1 small cauliflower, broken into florets

175 g (6 oz) fresh peas, podded (about 375 g/12 oz) in the pods

1 bunch of radishes, trimmed

4 spring onions, chopped

2 tablespoons chopped parsley

salt and pepper

mint sprigs, to garnish

Mint Dressing:

6 tablespoons mayonnaise

3 tablespoons natural yogurt

3 tablespoons water

½ garlic clove, crushed

1–2 tablespoons finely chopped mint

Serves 4–6

Preparation time: 20 minutes

Cooking time: about 10 minutes

mushroom & butter bean salad

1 Put the soaked beans in a large saucepan with plenty of cold water. Bring to the boil and boil briskly for 10 minutes, then lower the heat, cover and simmer for 30–40 minutes, until the beans are tender. Drain and rinse under cold running water, then drain thoroughly and leave to cool.

2 To make the dressing, stir together all the ingredients in a small bowl until blended, or shake the ingredients together in a screw-top jar until combined.

3 Thinly slice the mushrooms and place them in a large bowl. Add the cooled butter beans and pour the dressing over. Toss well to mix and leave to stand for at least 20 minutes before serving.

4 To serve, sprinkle the chives and parsley over the salad and toss lightly. If liked, use a potato peeler or a small sharp knife to pare wafer-thin slices of Parmesan over the top.

250 g (8 oz) dried butter beans, soaked overnight

250 g (8 oz) button mushrooms

1–2 tablespoons snipped chives

large handful of flat leaf parsley, roughly torn

50 g (2 oz) Parmesan cheese (optional)

Dressing:

5 tablespoons extra virgin olive oil

½ garlic clove, crushed

1 teaspoon finely grated lemon rind

2 tablespoons lemon juice

½ teaspoon Dijon mustard

pinch of sugar

salt and pepper

Serves 4–6

Preparation time: 15 minutes, plus soaking and standing

Cooking time: 40–50 minutes

cucumber & dill salad

1 Put the cucumber slices in a colander set over a large plate or in the sink. Sprinkle the salt over the cucumber and leave to stand for 20–30 minutes, to allow the excess moisture to drain away. Rinse the cucumber under cold running water, then drain thoroughly and place in a shallow serving dish.

2 To make the dressing, stir all the ingredients together in a small bowl.

3 Spoon the dressing over the cucumber and toss lightly to mix. Garnish with sprigs of dill and serve.

1 cucumber, peeled and very thinly sliced

2 teaspoons salt

sprigs of dill, to garnish

Dressing:

4 tablespoons thick natural yogurt or Greek yogurt

1 teaspoon white wine vinegar

2 tablespoons chopped dill

pepper

Serves 4–6

Preparation time: 15 minutes, plus standing

tuscan salad

1 Cook the rice in boiling salted water for 15 minutes, or until tender, or according to packet instructions. Drain well. Put in a mixing bowl and stir in the wine. Set aside to cool.

2 Put the green and red peppers, beans, cucumber, olives and spring onions in a salad bowl. When the rice is cold, add it to the vegetable mixture and stir well.

3 To make the dressing, whisk together all the ingredients in a small bowl until blended, or shake the ingredients together in a screw-top jar until combined. Add to the rice mixture and toss to coat thoroughly. Chill for 30 minutes, tossing occasionally. Serve garnished with basil sprigs.

250 g (8 oz) long-grain rice

4 tablespoons dry white wine

1 green pepper, cored, deseeded and thinly sliced

1 red pepper, cored, deseeded and thinly sliced

125 g (4 oz) canned fagioli or other beans, drained

1 small cucumber, peeled and diced

10 stuffed green olives

2 spring onions, thinly sliced

basil sprigs, to garnish

Dressing:

6 tablespoons olive oil

3 tablespoons red wine vinegar

1 teaspoon dried basil

1 garlic clove, peeled and crushed

1 teaspoon salt

½ teaspoon pepper

Serves 4

Preparation time: 15 minutes, plus cooling and chilling

Cooking time: 15 minutes

1 Heat the oil in a large saucepan and cook the onions and garlic gently for 5 minutes. Add the tomatoes and cook for a few minutes until the juice starts to flow.

2 Add the courgettes and aubergines and stir them all together to mix. Add salt and pepper to serve.

3 Cover the pan and simmer for about 30 minutes, or until the vegetables are softened.

4 Taste and adjust the seasoning if necessary, then stir in some of the chopped parsley. Serve with the remaining parsley sprinkled over the top and with some French bread.

4 tablespoons olive oil

3 onions, finely chopped

3 garlic cloves, finely chopped

750 g (1½ lb) tomatoes, skinned and chopped

5 courgettes, sliced

2 large aubergines, sliced

2 tablespoons chopped parsley

salt and pepper

French bread, to serve

Serves 6–8
Preparation time: 15–20 minutes
Cooking time: 1 hour

braised mediterranean vegetables

spiced okra

1 Heat the oil in a large frying
pan and fry the onion gently for
5 minutes, until softened. Stir in the
okra, coriander, chilli powder and salt
to taste. Cover and cook gently for
10 minutes.

2 Sprinkle with the garam masala
and lemon juice. Stir well to mix,
transfer to a heated serving dish and
serve immediately.

2 tablespoons sunflower oil

1 onion, chopped

500 g (1 lb) okra, trimmed and sliced

1 teaspoon ground coriander

½ teaspoon chilli powder

1 teaspoon garam masala

1 tablespoon lemon juice

salt

Serves 4
Preparation time: 10 minutes
Cooking time: 15 minutes

fresh mayonnaise

1 To make mayonnaise by hand, put the egg yolks into a mixing bowl and add the mustard and salt and pepper. Whisk to blend. Hold the container of oil and leave your 'working' hand free to whisk continually.

2 Add the oil in a very slow trickle, whisking all the time. If the mixture starts to curdle, stop adding the oil and whisk very hard. If that does not help, you will need to add another egg yolk. Beat this in and start adding the oil once again. The 2 egg yolks should absorb the quantity of oil specified, but for some people this gives too oily a dressing, so stop when sufficient has been incorporated. Add the vinegar or vinegar and lemon juice. The hot water lightens the dressing. Use the mayonnaise at once or cover and refrigerate for 2–3 days only.

3 To make mayonnaise in a food processor or blender, you can use whole eggs if liked. This makes a much lighter dressing than one made with just the yolks, but it means you cannot add so much oil.

4 Put the eggs into the goblet or bowl with the mustard, salt and pepper. Keep the motor running at the lowest speed possible. Gradually trickle in the oil through the feeding tube. When this has been incorporated, add the vinegar, vinegar and lemon juice and hot water.

2 egg yolks at room temperature

1 teaspoon Dijon mustard

300 ml (½ pint) virgin olive oil

1–2 tablespoons white wine vinegar or lemon juice, or a mixture of both

1 tablespoon very hot water (optional)

salt pepper

Serves 4–6

Preparation time: by hand, 20 minutes; using a food processor or blender, 5 minutes

■ This recipe can form the basis of any number of dressings. For garlic mayonnaise, add 4-5 crushed garlic cloves, for blue cheese dressing, incorporate 250 g (8 oz) crumbled Gorgonzola or dolcelatte, for green dressing, add 2 finely chopped spring onions and 25 g (1 oz) finely chopped watercress.

basic barbecue sauce

1 Mix all the ingredients together in a small saucepan and bring to the boil, use hot or cold.

4 tablespoons tomato ketchup

4 tablespoons brown fruity sauce

1 teaspoon English mustard

1 tablespoon Worcestershire sauce

1 tablespoon brown sugar

Serves 3–4

Preparation time: 5 minutes

herb marinade

1 Mix together all the ingredients in a bowl with salt and pepper to taste, or place in a screw-top jar and shake well.

4 tablespoons sunflower oil

2 tablespoons lemon juice

1 teaspoon chopped marjoram

1 teaspoon chopped thyme

2 tablespoons chopped parsley

1 garlic clove, crushed

1 onion, finely chopped

salt and pepper

Serves 4

Preparation time: 5 minutes

grilled fruit skewers with coconut custard •

lemon & passion fruit tart •

ginger cheesecake •

melon & rosewater granita •

st clement's ice cream •

apricot sorbet •

baked blueberry purses with almond cream •

raspberry cheesecake •

chocolate & pine nut meringue stack •

desserts

grilled fruit skewers with coconut custard

1 First make the coconut custard. Whisk the egg yolks and sugar in a bowl until thick and creamy. Mix the coconut milk and cream in a saucepan and bring to just below boiling point, then pour into the beaten egg yolk mixture, whisking constantly. Pour the mixture into a clean pan. Place over a low heat and stir constantly until the mixture coats the back of a spoon. Be careful not to let the mixture boil or the custard will curdle. Remove the pan from the heat and immediately strain the custard into a bowl. Stir in the rum or liqueur, if using, and cover tightly. When cool, chill the custard in the refrigerator.

2 Prepare the fruit and cut it into even-sized pieces. Thread on to 8 presoaked wooden or oiled metal skewers, to create a colourful effect. Brush with lime or lemon juice. Cook on the oiled grill of a preheated barbecue for 2–3 minutes on each side, then sprinkle the fruit with the sugar and cook the skewers for 1 minute more. Serve immediately, with a separate bowl of coconut custard for dipping, like a cold fondue.

1 kg (2 lb) assorted fruits in season (e.g. mango, papaya, peach, strawberries, oranges, apples or pears)

lime or lemon juice, for brushing

2 tablespoons muscovado or caster sugar

Coconut Custard:

4 egg yolks

75 g (3 oz) caster sugar

150 ml (¼ pint) coconut milk

150 ml (¼ pint) double cream

1 tablespoon rum, Cointreau or other liqueur (optional)

Serves 4

Preparation time: 25 minutes, plus chilling

Cooking time: 4–6 minutes

■ Coconut milk is available from supermarkets and oriental food stores. It is not the same as the 'milk' found inside a fresh coconut.

lemon & passion fruit tart

1 Place the flour in the bowl, add the butter and rub in with the fingertips until the mixture resembles fine breadcrumbs. Stir in the sugar, then add about 2 tablespoons of water and mix to a firm dough. Wrap in clingfilm and chill for 15 minutes.

2 Roll out the dough and line a 20 cm (8 inch) fluted flan tin. Trim off the excess pastry. Line with grease-proof paper and fill with baking beans. Bake in a preheated oven, 200ºC (400ºF), Gas Mark 6, for 15 minutes. Remove the beans and paper and cook for a further 5 minutes. Reduce the oven to 160ºC (325ºF), Gas Mark 3.

3 Make the filling. Beat together the eggs and sugar, then stir in the cream, lemon rind and juice. Pour into the tart case and bake for 25–30 minutes, until just set. Leave to cool.

4 Whip the cream until it just holds its shape. Serve the tart with the cream on top and scoop the seeds from the passion fruit on to the cream, to decorate.

Pastry:

175 g (6 oz) plain flour

125 g (4 oz) butter, diced

25 g (1 oz) caster sugar

Filling:

4 eggs

125 g (4 oz) caster sugar

150 ml (¼ pint) double cream

grated rind and juice of 3 lemons

150 ml (¼ pint) double cream, to serve

3 passion fruit, halved, to decorate

Serves 8

Preparation time: 25 minutes, plus chilling

Cooking time: 40–45 minutes

ginger cheesecake

1 Melt the butter in a saucepan. Remove from the heat and mix in the biscuit crumbs and ginger. Press on to the base and sides of a 20 cm (8 inch) flan dish.

2 To make the filling, place the cheese in a bowl and blend in the yogurt, egg yolks and sugar. Stir in the ginger and syrup. Whisk the egg whites until stiff and fold into the cheese mixture. Pour into the flan case and sprinkle with grated nutmeg.

3 Bake in a preheated moderate oven, 160°C (325°F), Gas Mark 3, for 20–25 minutes until firm and golden. Allow to cool, then chill.

4 Whip the cream until thick. Decorate the cheesecake with piped whipped cream and ginger slices before serving.

75 g (3 oz) butter

175 g (6 oz) digestive biscuits, crushed

1 tablespoon ground ginger

Filling:

250 g (8 oz) medium fat curd cheese

2 tablespoons natural yogurt

2 eggs, separated

2 tablespoons soft brown sugar

2 pieces stem ginger, finely chopped

1 tablespoon ginger syrup (from jar)

grated nutmeg

To Decorate:

150 ml (¼ pint) double cream

stem ginger slices

Serves 6

Preparation time: 20 minutes, plus cooling and chilling

Cooking time: 20–25 minutes

melon & rosewater granita

1 Cut the melons in half, remove the seeds and scoop out the flesh into a food processor or blender.

2 Place the sugar and measured water in a saucepan and heat for about 1–2 minutes, until the sugar has dissolved. Increase the heat and boil for another 2 minutes without stirring, then remove from the heat and leave to cool slightly.

3 Add half the sugar syrup to the melon flesh and blend until smooth. Pour into a bowl and stir in the rosewater and more sugar syrup to taste; the amount needed will depend on the sweetness of the fruit.

4 Pour the melon mixture into a 25 x 15 cm (10 x 6 inch) tin and place it in the refrigerator to chill. When the mixture is cold, transfer the tin to the freezer for about 1 hour, or until ice crystals have formed around the rim and the mixture is starting to freeze on the base. Scrape the mixture with a fork, combining with any liquid, then replace in the freezer. Repeat every 45 minutes for about 4–5 hours, until uniform crystals have formed. Serve within 4–6 hours.

2 Charentais or rock melons

75 g (3 oz) caster sugar

175 ml (6 fl oz) water

½ teaspoon rosewater

Serves 4–6
Preparation time: 10 minutes
Cooking time: about 5 minutes
Freezing time: 5–6 hours

■ Cool and refreshing, granitas are the ideal barbecue dessert. They can be prepared in advance and kept in the freezer until required.

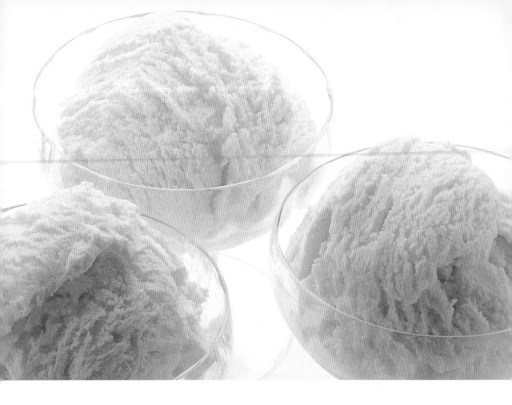

st clement's ice cream

1 Whisk together the egg yolks, half the sugar and the lemon and orange rinds until thick and creamy. Strain the fruit juices into a saucepan and heat gently, then pour on to the egg mixture and continue whisking until thick.

2 Whisk the egg whites until stiff, then whisk in the remaining sugar. Fold into the egg mixture with the cream.

3 Turn the mixture into a rigid freezerproof container. Cover and freeze until firm. This will take about 5–6 hours.

4 Transfer the ice cream to the refrigerator 30 minutes before serving to soften. Scoop into chilled glasses and serve with wafer biscuits, if liked.

3 eggs, separated

175 g (6 oz) caster sugar

grated rind and juice of 1 lemon

grated rind and juice of 1 orange

300 ml (½ pint) double cream, whipped

wafer biscuits, to serve (optional)

Serves 6–8
Preparation time: 20 minutes
Cooking time: 2–4 minutes
Freezing time: 5–6 hours

apricot sorbet

1 Place the apricots in a saucepan with 150 ml (¼ pint) of the water. Cover and simmer gently for about 15 minutes, until tender. Cool slightly, then put the apricots into a food processor or blender with the lime or lemon juice and process until smooth.

2 Heat the remaining water and the sugar gently in a heavy-based saucepan, stirring constantly until the sugar has dissolved. Bring to the boil and boil rapidly for 5 minutes, then stir into the apricot purée and leave to cool completely.

3 Add the kirsch or brandy and pour the mixture into a rigid freezerproof container. Cover and freeze for 2–3 hours, until half-frozen. Remove from the freezer and turn into a bowl. Whisk the egg white until stiff, then whisk into the half-frozen apricot mixture. Return the sorbet to the freezer container, cover and freeze.

4 Transfer the sorbet to the refrigerator 10 minutes before serving to soften. Scoop into chilled glasses, decorate with borage sprigs and serve immediately.

500 g (1 lb) fresh apricots, stoned

450 ml (¾ pint) water

juice of ½ lime or lemon

175 g (6 oz) granulated sugar

2 tablespoons kirsch or apricot brandy

1 egg white

borage sprigs, to decorate

Serves 6–8

Preparation time: 10 minutes, plus cooling

Cooking time: about 25 minutes

Freezing time: 5–6 hours

■ If wished, you could substitute blackcurrants for the apricots and crème de cassis for the kirsch.

baked blueberry purses with almond cream

1 To make the almond cream, first line an 18 cm (7 inch) sieve with a piece of muslin large enough to over-hang the edge by about 10 cm (4 inches). Place the lined sieve over a bowl.

2 In a mixing bowl, beat the ground almonds with the mascarpone. In a separate bowl, beat the egg yolks with the sugar until pale and fluffy. Fold into the mascarpone mixture.

3 Whip the cream in another bowl until it forms soft peaks. Fold into the mascarpone with the Amaretto. Turn the mixture into the lined sieve, fold the excess muslin over, cover with a small plate and set a small weight on top. Place in the refrigerator for 6–8 hours or overnight to drain.

4 The blueberries are cooked in individual foil purses. For each purse you will require a 33 cm (13 inch) square of double foil. Heap a quarter of the blueberries in the cen-tre of each foil square and turn up the edges to form a lip. Sprinkle the blue-berries with 1 tablespoon of the vanilla sugar. Drizzle 1 tablespoon of the crème de cassis over the top, bring up the edges of the foil to make a purse and press together to seal. Cook the sealed foil purses on the oiled grill of a preheated barbecue for 8–10 minutes.

5 Unmould the almond cream on to a large plate. Serve portions of the almond cream beside the blueber-ries and jug of single cream, if liked.

750 g (1½ lb) fresh blueberries
6–8 tablespoons vanilla sugar
6–8 tablespoons crème de cassis
single cream, to serve (optional)

Almond Cream:
750 g (1½ lb) ground almonds
1 kg (2 lb) mascarpone cream
3 egg yolks
125 g (4 oz) caster sugar
125 ml (4 fl oz) double cream
2 tablespoons Amaretto

Serves 6–8

Preparation time: 15 minutes, plus draining

Cooking time: 10 minutes

raspberry cheesecake

1 Melt the butter or margarine in a small pan, then remove from the heat and mix in the biscuit crumbs. Press the mixture over the base of a lightly oiled 20 cm (8 inch) springform cake tin; chill in the refrigerator for about 15 minutes until firm.

2 Put the cheese in a bowl and beat in the sugar and egg yolks. Whip the cream until it will stand in soft peaks. Stir the dissolved gelatine into the cheese mixture, then fold in the cream.

3 Whisk the egg whites until stiff, then fold 2 tablespoons into the cheese mixture to lighten it. Fold in the remaining egg whites, then spoon the mixture over the biscuit base and level the surface. Chill the cheesecake in the refrigerator for 1–1½ hours or until the filling is set.

4 Pipe a whipped cream border around the edge of the cheese-cake and arrange the raspberries over the top. Serve the cheesecake chilled.

50 g (2 oz) butter or margarine

125 g (4 oz) digestive biscuits, crushed

375 g (12 oz) curd cheese

50 g (2 oz) caster sugar

3 eggs, separated

300 ml (½ pint) double cream

15 g (½ oz) powdered gelatine, dissolved in 3 tablespoons of orange juice

To Serve:

4 tablespoons double cream, whipped

250 g (8 oz) raspberries

Serves 6–8

Preparation time: 20 minutes, plus chilling

chocolate & pine nut meringue stack

1 Line 4 baking sheets with non-stick baking paper. Draw a 20 cm (8 inch) circle on each one.

2 Sift the cocoa powder and icing sugar into a small bowl. Place the egg whites and salt in a separate, greasefree bowl and whisk until stiff. Gradually whisk in the caster sugar, 1 tablespoon at a time. Fold in the icing sugar mixture and chopped pine nuts until evenly combined.

3 Divide the meringue mixture evenly between the circles on the baking sheets and spread out with a palette knife. Place in a preheated oven, 150°C (300°F), Gas Mark 2, and bake for 1–1¼ hours. Remove from the oven and cool on wire racks.

4 Make the Marsala cream. Whisk the egg yolks, caster sugar and Marsala in a bowl until creamy, then beat in the mascarpone until well combined. Place the egg whites in a separate, greasefree bowl and whisk until stiff, then fold into the mascarpone mixture.

5 Divide the Marsala cream between 3 of the meringue bases, spreading it to the edges. Stack these meringues on top of each other on a serving plate, then crush the last layer into small pieces and sprinkle on top. Place the dessert in the refrigerator for 2–4 hours. Serve dusted with icing sugar and cocoa powder.

50 g (2 oz) cocoa powder

125 g (4 oz) icing sugar

6 egg whites

pinch of salt

175 g (6 oz) caster sugar

125 g (4 oz) pine nuts, toasted and chopped

icing sugar and cocoa powder, to decorate

Marsala Cream:

2 eggs, separated

2 tablespoons caster sugar

2 tablespoons Marsala

500 g (1 lb) mascarpone cheese

Serves 8–10
Preparation time: 35 minutes, plus chilling
Cooking time: 1–1¼ hours

index